Children of
YUCATÁN

THE WORLD'S CHILDREN

Children of YUCATÁN

written and photographed by
FRANK STAUB

Carolrhoda Books, Inc./Minneapolis

For my Philadelphia family

Many thanks to Rosie Garcia for sharing her knowledge of Yucatán.

Text and photographs © 1996 by Carolrhoda Books, Inc.
Additional photographs on pp. 18 (left) and 25 (left) © Chuck Place.
Map on p. 9 by John Erste © 1996 by Carolrhoda Books, Inc.

Carolrhoda Books, Inc. c/o The Lerner Group
241 First Avenue North, Minneapolis, MN 55401

LIBRARY OF CONGRESS CATALOGING-IN-PUBLICATION DATA
Staub, Frank J.
    Children of Yucatán / by Frank Staub.
        p. cm. — (The world's children)
    Includes index.
    Summary: Describes life in Yucatán, Mexico, focusing on the daily activities and cultural history of some modern Mayan children.
    ISBN 0-87614-984-0
    1. Maya children—Mexico—Yucatán (State)—Juvenile literature. 2. Mayas—Social life and customs—Juvenile literature. 3. Mayas—Antiquities—Juvenile literature. 4. Yucatán (Mexico : State)—Social life and customs—Juvenile literature. 5. Yucatán (Mexico : State)—Antiquities—Juvenile literature. [1. Mayas—Social life and customs. 2. Indians of Mexico—Social life and customs. 3. Yucatán (Mexico : State)—Social life and customs.] I. Title. II. Series: World's children (Minneapolis, Minn.)
F1435.3 C47S73 1996
972'.65—dc20   95-35027

Manufactured in the United States of America
1 2 3 4 5 6 – JR – 01 00 99 98 97 96

Early morning in Izamal

Above: *Guadalupe and her mother*
Right: *A traditional Mayan* na

The sun is up in Izamal, and Guadalupe is dressed for school. As she waits in the yard for her friends to come by, her mother brushes her long, dark hair. Guadalupe and her mom are Maya Indians. The Maya have lived in what is now Mexico and Central America for thousands of years. Much of their culture has been lost. But many modern Maya still live in traditional Mayan houses called *nas*.

A *na* stays fairly cool, because doors in the front and back let the breeze blow through. Clay in the walls and tough palm leaves in the thatched roof also help keep out the heat.

A cool house is important in this part of the world. This is the tropics, where the weather can get very hot and humid.

Guadalupe lives in Izamal, in the Mexican state of Yucatán. Yucatán is part of the United States of Mexico, at the end of the Yucatán Peninsula. (A peninsula is a piece of land that juts out into a body of water.)

Most of Yucatán is flat and covered with short trees and thorny bushes. Beaches, swamps, and marshes line Yucatán's long coast.

Almost all the people who live in Yucatán have some Mayan ancestors. In the 1500s, explorers from Spain invaded Mexico and ruled Yucatán until 1821. Many Spaniards settled in Yucatán during that time and married Maya. People with both Indian and European ancestors are called mestizos. Ninety percent of the people in Yucatán are either Maya or mestizo. Most of the others are of Spanish ancestry.

Julio and his dad, Henry, are going to get gasoline for their fishing boat. Most of their ancestors were from Europe.

Mauricio is descended from Maya Indians. He is swimming in one of Mexico's many cenotes. *A* cenote *is a pool of water formed when the roof of a flooded cave falls in.*

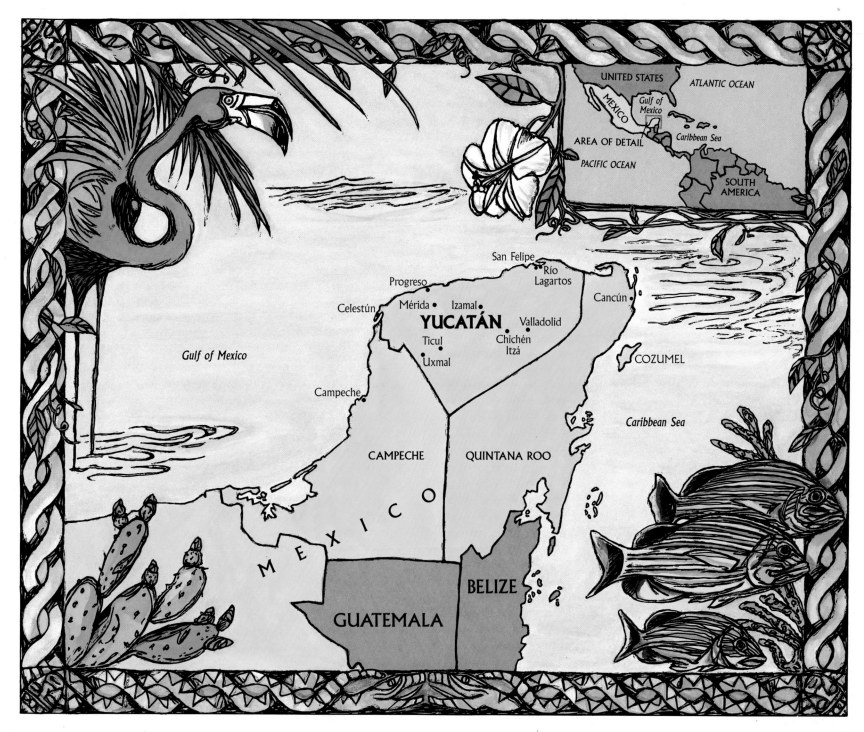

UNITED STATES

ATLANTIC OCEAN

MEXICO

Gulf of Mexico

AREA OF DETAIL

Caribbean Sea

PACIFIC OCEAN

SOUTH AMERICA

San Felipe

Progreso

Río Lagartos

Celestún

Mérida   Izamal

Cancún

YUCATÁN

Valladolid

Ticul

Chichén Itzá

Gulf of Mexico

Uxmal

COZUMEL

Campeche

Caribbean Sea

CAMPECHE   QUINTANA ROO

M E X I C O

BELIZE

GUATEMALA

It is afternoon in Izamal, and a storm is building. Afternoon rainstorms are common in the tropics. They move in quickly. It may be sunny one minute and raining the next. Selny, Juan, and Rubi get home from school before the storm hits.

Across the street from their house is a hill with a secret. Under the trees, bushes, and soil stands a huge stone pyramid. It was built by the ancient Maya hundreds of years before the Spaniards came.

A storm looms over the Convento de San Antonio de Padua, one of many Catholic churches built with stones from Mayan pyramids.

In another part of town, the rain has already begun. As Eduardo pedals his bike home, he passes two pyramids that have been uncovered by archaeologists. Archaeologists study ancient people by looking at the things they left behind.

Not all ancient buildings in Yucatán are still standing. When the Spaniards came to Mexico, they used stones from pyramids to build Catholic churches. Then they forced the Maya to become Christians. In modern-day Yucatán, almost everyone is Catholic.

Eduardo races past a Mayan pyramid.

Selny, Juan, and Rubi in front of a hill of buried ruins

11

Bertha and her friends are students at a private Catholic school in Izamal. Most Mexican children attend public schools, which are paid for by the government. Public schools are divided into elementary, middle, and high schools, just like schools in the United States. Children are required to attend school from ages six to fourteen. Subjects include math, history, geography, natural science, art, and physical education. Elementary school students also study Spanish grammar and spelling. Spanish is the official language of Mexico.

The school day lasts from 8:00 or 9:00 in the morning until 2:00 in the afternoon, every day except weekends. Summer vacation is the month of August.

Despite the law, about half of all Mexican children quit school before they turn fourteen. Most of them go to work to help support their families.

Above: *After the rain stops, Bertha and her friends decide to play in their school's huge front courtyard. Bertha goes for the ball.* Right: *Izamal is called "the Yellow City" because it has lots of yellow buildings. This is a hardware store.*

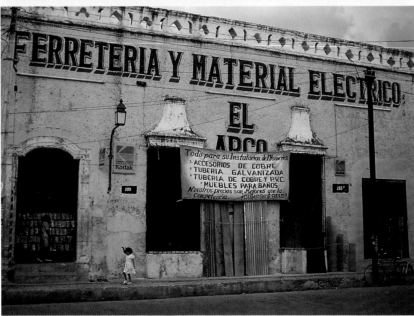

Left: *Carriages called victorias are used like taxis to travel around Izamal.* Below: *English is not taught during the normal school day, so these students stay late for a special class.*

Fredi is fifteen years old and doesn't go to school anymore. He works in a feed store in Izamal. He gets paid in pesos, the official money of Mexico. Fredi doesn't make a lot of money, but he's glad to have a job. Many people in Mexico are unemployed.

Feed stores like the one where Fredi works are usually busy, because many people in Yucatán own pigs, chickens, or cows. Gustavo, Wendy, and Elsa keep a pig in their backyard. Its name is Orky. Some day Orky will be killed for food. But in the meantime, he is treated like a pet.

This morning, Orky was so hungry that he started to nibble on Gustavo's hair. Then Wendy came out with Orky's food.

Fredi carries a bag of pig feed for a customer.

14

Orky nibbles Gustavo's hair until Wendy brings breakfast.

15

Carlos stands in front of a henequén *plant.*

16

Each morning on his way to school, Carlos walks past a field of *henequén*. The large leaves of the *henequén* plant yield tough, stringy fibers that can be made into rope, twine, bags, hammocks, and other products. *Henequén* plants store water in their leaves, so they grow well in Yucatán's dry soil.

In the late 1800s, the people of Yucatán grew wealthy as they filled the world's need for rope. Then other countries started growing *henequén,* and Yucatán's farmers couldn't sell as much as they had before. In the 1920s, nylon and other human-made fibers were invented, and the demand for natural rope dropped. However, *henequén* is still Yucatán's main crop. Products made of *henequén* can be found in markets all around Yucatán.

Above: Henequén *fibers can be up to five feet long.* Left: Henequén *rope for sale*

17

Some markets have roofs over them, but many are out in the open.

Beef is one of many foods sold in Yucatán's markets.

Markets are an important part of life in Yucatán. People go to their local marketplace to buy and sell meat, fruits, and vegetables, and to visit with their neighbors.

Victor hauls containers of tortillas and beans to sell at the market. A tortilla is a piece of thin, round bread made from wheat or corn flour. Mexicans put beef, chicken, turkey, vegetables, or beans on them and roll them up to make Mexican-style sandwiches called tacos.

Mexicans can also shop for clothing, housewares, and other items at the markets. Many of these items are made locally. The factory where Ángel works is famous for its beautiful bowls and other products made from the wood of the huaya-can tree.

People in Yucatán also shop in stores and on the sidewalks. Sidewalk vendors can make walking difficult, because the sidewalks are often narrow.

Above: *Victor uses a three-wheeled cycle to haul food to the market.*
Left: *Ángel carves decorations on the outside of a bowl.*

Hilaria and her grandchildren are enjoying one of Yucatán's favorite foods—fresh, juicy oranges.

Fernando knows well how much people like Mexico's oranges. He sells them to hungry passersby in the city of Valladolid. Fernando peels the fruit so his customers can suck out the juice more easily. He is proud of his mechanical peeler because it saves him time and work.

Nearby, Juan earns money for his family by shining shoes in the plaza, or park, in the center of Valladolid. Valladolid's plaza has a lot in common with plazas in other cities in Yucatán. It's next to the biggest and oldest church in town, and it's a place for friends to meet and for children to play. It can also be a place to talk business. On Sunday evenings, Yucatán's plazas come alive, because that's when people get dressed up and come downtown.

Left: *Hilaria and her grandchildren.* Above: *Fernando and his orange peeler*

20

Above: *Sunday night is dress-up time at town plazas all around Yucatán. This one is in the city of Ticul.* Right: *Juan shines shoes in the town plaza.*

Rosario and Luseli come to Valladolid's plaza on weekends to make some money. They sell doll dresses that look like the *huipil* Rosario is wearing.

The Maya are world famous for their beautiful *huipils*. It can take weeks to stitch the designs of colorful flowers and birds on a single dress. You can tell which village a woman comes from by the designs on her *huipil*. Sometimes the designs have religious or even magical meanings. A look around the plaza shows that many Mayan women have given up *huipils* for modern dresses.

One thing that many Mayans haven't given up is the Mayan language. There are about 20 different forms of the Mayan language in Mexico and Central America. Rosario and Luseli speak both Mayan and Spanish. In rural Yucatán, some Maya speak no Spanish at all.

Rosario and Luseli sell doll-size huipils *in the town plaza.*

Some Mayan women and girls still wear huipils. But most Mayan men and boys wear modern clothing.

It's Sunday, and Aliseli, Gladys, and Carlos have come to Valladolid's plaza. Like many brothers and sisters in Yucatán, they are close friends who look out for each other.

Family life is important in Yucatán. Grandparents often live in the same house with their children and grandchildren.

Even when family members die, they aren't forgotten. Cemeteries in Yucatán and the rest of Mexico are well cared for, and the grave markers are often decorated with bright colors.

In Mexico, November second is a national holiday called *el día de los muertos,* or Day of the Dead. All over the country, people have fiestas, or parties, at cemeteries to honor their dead relatives. Some believe the spirits of their relatives are present at the celebrations.

Aliseli, Gladys, and Carlos

24

On the Day of the Dead, family and friends remember a loved one who died June 10, 1984.

A seaside cemetery

One reason the people of Yucatán treat their ancestors with such respect is that they have provided their grandchildren with an important source of income. People come from all over the world to see the wonderful stone structures the ancient Maya left behind. And when visitors come, they spend money on food, hotels, and souvenirs.

In the Puuc hills of southern Yucatán stands what's left of the great city of Uxmal. The Maya built Uxmal between about A.D. 700 and 1000. Their *nas* fell down and rotted away long ago. But the great stone temples and pyramids are still there. These buildings were used as religious sites and as tombs for rulers and other important people.

By about A.D. 900, the people of Uxmal started to leave. No one is really sure why. Slowly the trees, bushes, and forest creatures took over the city.

Below: *Tourists visit Yucatán to see the great structures built by the ancient Maya.* Opposite page, top left: *While they are visiting, tourists often buy locally made souvenirs such as Panama hats.*

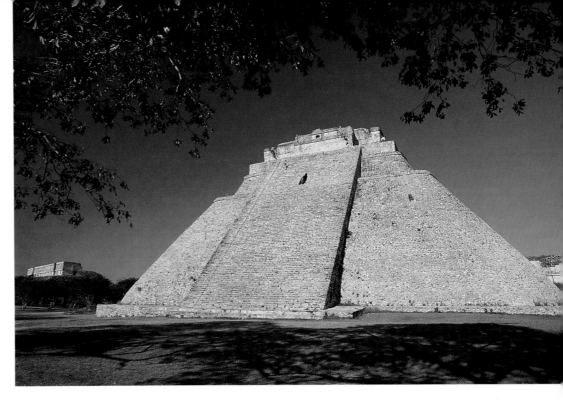

Above: *The tallest structure at Uxmal is the Pirámide del Adivino, or Pyramid of the Magician. Legend says it was built by a dwarf in just one night, as if by magic.* Left: *Many Mayan structures reflect the builders' knowledge of the skies. The Palacio del Gobenador, or Governor's Palace, was built so that in the year 750, the planet Venus would be visible through the doorway.*

El Castillo is another structure built with the study of the sky in mind. On the first day of spring and the first day of fall, the sun casts a shadow in the shape of a serpent on the side of the north staircase.

Slightly older than Uxmal, Chichén Itzá was the Maya's cultural, religious, and political center in ancient times. It is also the biggest Mayan city in Yucatán that archaeologists have uncovered so far.

For Alfredo and Rosendo, Chichén Itzá is a good place to make money for their families. Their fathers carve statues and little pyramids out of wood and stone for the boys to sell to tourists. Business is good, because thousands of people visit Chichén Itzá each year. Many of these tourists want to own something made by descendants of the great pyramid builders.

The pyramids the boys sell are models of El Castillo, one of the tallest pyramids in all of Yucatán. It was built around A.D. 800 and has a temple on top. A staircase runs up each of the pyramid's four sides. Each staircase contains 91 steps, for a total of 364. If the platform on the top is added, there are 365—one step for each day of the year.

Left: *Rosendo and Alfredo sell souvenirs to tourists.* Above: *The carved stone on ancient Mayan buildings was not meant just for decoration. The carvings are the Maya's written language and tell of Mayan religion and history.*

Left: *Adrian explores the Temple of the Warriors with his dad and his sister, Genny. Below: Jaguars are often found in ancient Mayan art. In this carving, the jaguar is eating a human heart.*

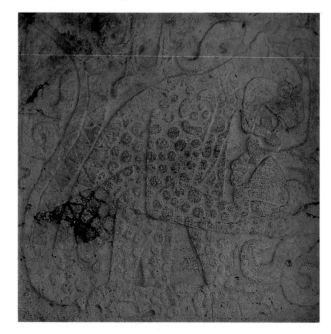

Inside El Castillo is a statue of a big cat called a jaguar. For the ancient Maya, jaguars were symbols of strength. Adrian Balam and his family are interested in jaguars because Balam means "jaguar" in Mayan. Adrian's dad, Benjamin, was born in Yucatán. But now the family lives on the island of Cozumel, in the neighboring state of Quintana Roo, where they own a store.

As Adrian walks down the steps of the Temple of the Warriors, he notices how nicely the stones fit together. He learned in school that the Maya didn't have horses or wheels to help move the big stones. They didn't even have metal tools. These things all came later, when the Spanish arrived. It must have taken the strength of thousands of people to build a great city like Chichén Itzá.

Above: *The Maya worshipped the rain god, Chac, for water to raise their crops. The reclining figure of Chac is common in Mayan art and architecture.* Left: *To contact Chac, the people of Chichén Itzá threw pottery, jewelry, and people into the Sacred Cenote. Did the Maya make human sacrifices? Or did they throw bodies into the water after people died naturally? No one knows.*

Right: *Uxmal's ball court is about the size of a tennis court, and the ring is several feet across.* Opposite page: *The main ball court at Chichén Itzá (one of eight in the city) is about the size of a football field, yet the ring (inset) isn't much bigger than a basketball hoop.*

Some of the most fascinating structures in the ancient Mayan cities are the ball courts. Mayan ball games were played by hitting the ball with one's elbows, knees, and hips. The players weren't allowed to touch the ball with their hands or feet. The goals were two stone rings on the side walls of the ball court. The game ended when one team hit the ball through the ring. Some Mayan ball games went on for days.

Pictures on the walls of the largest court at Chichén Itzá show players getting their heads cut off. The losing captain and possibly his whole team may have been sacrificed to the gods after big games.

Except for the violent ending, the Mayan ball game is like a combination of basketball and soccer. While children in Yucatán play both games, soccer is the favorite of most. Mexicans call soccer *fútbol,* which means football.

Young people play soccer in a churchyard in Ticul.

Baseball is Yucatán's second most popular sport, after soccer. Jorge and Roman take turns throwing a baseball on a string. This makes batting practice easy when there aren't enough people around to have a game.

Wendy plays third base on her school baseball team. Her friend Magaly plays catcher. Baseball came to Yucatán from the United States. That's not surprising, since Yucatán is only about 500 miles from Florida across the Gulf of Mexico. During the 1840s, Yucatán's leaders considered trying to become a state in the United States of America.

While Wendy and Magaly play catch, they hear music drifting out of Rosa's house. It's a classic rock-and-roll tune from the 1950s, "Rock around the Clock," and it came from the United States too. It is one of Rosa's favorite songs. She can't understand the words, because she speaks only Spanish. But some of her older friends can. They are learning English so they can do business with American tourists.

Jorge pitches with a ball on a string so he doesn't have to chase after it every time Roman gets a hit.

Left: *Wendy and Magaly.* Above: *Rosa dances in her yard.*

The children who live along Yucatán's coast are lucky because they can play in or on the water all year long. Luis lives in the coastal town of San Felipe. He wears a mask to check out what's underwater. Many different kinds of fish live there. Much of the bottom is sandy or rocky. Yucatán lacks the beautiful coral reefs found along the coast of Quintana Roo, on the east side of the Yucatán Peninsula.

At the other end of the dock, some girls are playing on an overturned rowboat. The girls have lived next to the water all their lives, so they learned how to swim at an early age. Many years ago, children swimming in Yucatán's waters had to watch out for alligators. But almost all of the alligators in the area have been killed for their meat and skins.

Luis's mask keeps water out of his eyes so he can get a clearer view of the fish.

The swimming is fine in San Felipe.

Catching creatures from the sea is an important way to make a living in Yucatán. It requires a lot of work, even for the children. In San Felipe, Mayra uses a net to catch little fish for her father to use as bait. Tomorrow he will travel miles from shore to catch barracuda and other kinds of fish.

Most ocean fishers use

Mayra

large nets to make their catch. In Celestún, José helps his uncle Moisés get a new net ready for use.

In Celestún and in Río Lagartos to the east, fishers don't use their boats just for fishing. They also take people to see the flamingos. These bird-watching trips help many fishers get by when the fishing is poor.

Sometimes boats get too close and scare the birds away. Seeing hundreds of pink birds fly up all at once is a thrill. But if the flamingos are scared away too many times, they may not come back.

Above: *Río Lagartos is home to the largest number of flamingos in North America.* Left: *José and Moisés*

Despite Yucatán's long coastline, there is only one place in the whole state where big, modern ships can dock—the city of Progreso. The ocean is very shallow along the Yucatán coast, so Progreso's wharf is four miles long. It stretches out to where the water is deep enough for large ships. The wharf is so big that cars and trucks can drive on it.

Many people who go to Progreso's beach head for the wharf. Fishers often cast their nets near the wharf to catch some of the many fish that live in the water below it.

It is sunny and warm, and Raúl and his daughter Alejandra are enjoying a day at the beach. Under a small dock, they look for little crab-like animals called *huche*. *Huche* live in the sand where the waves break. Not far away, students from the Carlos Marx School spend gym class on the beach.

Left: *Raúl and Alejandra dig for* huche. Below: *Children from the Carlos Marx School feed the seagulls.*

Opposite page: *Progreso's wharf*

41

The Spaniards built their churches and cathedrals to be very strong. The Spaniards had reason to be afraid. They had taken land and destroyed property belonging to the Maya. More than once, the Maya fought back.

Progreso was built as a seaport for Mérida, the Yucatán state capital 22 miles away. With well over half a million people, Mérida is the largest city in southern Mexico.

Almost everyone who visits Yucatán comes to Mérida. They come to buy crafts such as hammocks and Panama hats. They also come to see Mérida's great cathedral. Built by the Spaniards from 1556 to 1599, it is probably the oldest cathedral in North America. As with the church in Izamal, many of its stones were taken from a Mayan pyramid.

Local people visit Mérida's cathedral to pray. Sometimes people who have no money sit on the sidewalk in front of the cathedral's great doors, waiting for someone to hand them a coin. Tere works outside the cathedral. She sells icons, rosary beads, and other religious products to the cathedral's visitors.

A man holds out a cup for coins.

Tere at work, with her boss Alfio

Mérida can be a fun place to live or to visit, because with so many people there's always something to do. In the central plaza, you can see entertainment almost every night.

Rosie and her friends are part of a children's dance group called the Ballet Infantil. They will perform tonight with other groups in similar costumes. The women wear Mayan *huipils*. The men wear white pants and shirts and broad-brimmed hats, typical of the Spanish settlers.

Carlos has a jar of soapy liquid. He blows bubbles from a balcony of the Palacio del Gobierno, Yucatán's state capitol building. The bubbles drift across the street and toward the plaza. Down below, the dancing is beginning.

Left: *Carlos blows bubbles from the balcony of the Palacio del Gobierno.*
Below: *Rosie (second from left) and friends*

MORE ABOUT YUCATÁN

How big is Yucatán?
Yucatán covers about 15,000 square miles. That's roughly the size of Delaware and Maryland combined.

What does "Yucatán" mean?
The word *Yucatán* comes from the Mayan word *Ci-u-thán,* which means "We don't understand each other." That's what the Maya said to the first Europeans they met.

MORE ABOUT THE MAYA

Where do the Maya live?
The ancient Maya lived in what is now southern Mexico, Guatemala, Belize, Honduras, and El Salvador. The modern Maya live mainly on the Yucatán Peninsula, in the Mexican state of Chiapas, and in Guatemala and Belize.

How many Maya are there?
There are over two million Maya alive today.

How long did the ancient Mayan civilization last?
From about 2000 B.C. to the arrival of the Spaniards in the mid-1500s A.D.—roughly 3,500 years.

What were some of the important achievements of the ancient Maya?
The ancient Maya had the most advanced civilization in the Americas before the Europeans came. They made important discoveries in astronomy, mathematics, and the making of calendars. They developed one of the first written languages. The Maya also left behind beautiful examples of architecture, pottery, painting, sculpture, and literature.

PRONUNCIATION GUIDE

Celestún sell-es-TOON
cenote say-NO-tay
Chichén Itzá CHEE-chen EET-sa
El Castillo EL cah-STEE-yoh
el día de los muertos EL DEE-ah DAY
   LOHS MWAYR-tohs
henequén eh-neh-KAYN
huche WAH-chay
huipil we-PEEL
Izamal EE-zuh-mall
Maya MY-uh
Mérida MAY-ree-dah
mestizo may-STEET-so
na NAH
Progreso pro-GRAY-so
San Felipe SAHN fay-LEE-pay
Ticul TEE-cool
tortilla tor-TEE-yuh
Uxmal OOSH-mall
Valladolid by-yah-doh-LEET
Yucatán yoo-kuh-TAHN

Index